D11199314

PEOPLE AT
THE CENTER OF

THE
KOREAN WAR

By ROB EDELMAN

BLACKBIRCH PRESS

An imprint of Thomson Gale, a part of The Thomson Corporation

Detroit • New York • San Francisco • San Diego • New Haven, Conn. • Waterville, Maine • London • Munich

Picture credits: Cover: © Hulton Archive by Getty Images (main); © Time-Life Pictures by Getty Images, © Hulton Archive by Getty Images, © AFP/Getty Images, Landov (cover portraits); © Bettmann/CORBIS, 18, 22, 26–27, 28, 31, 32, 34, 36, 42, 43; © Blackbirch Press, 40; © Time-Life Pictures by Getty Images, 14; © CORBIS, 19; Courtesy of U.S. Army, 10; Courtesy of Harry S. Truman Library, 17; © Handout/Reuters/CORBIS, 13; © Hulton-Deutsch Collection/CORBIS, 25, 37; Library of Congress, 5, 9, 11, 38; National Archives, 6–7, 15, 29; © Bill White, 21; Steve Zmina, 39

LIBRARY OF CONGRESS CATALOGING-IN-PUBLICATION DATA

Edelman, Rob.
  The Korean War / by Rob Edelman.
    p. cm. — (People at the center of:)
  Summary: Profiles people involved in the Korean War as soldiers and politicians, including Harry S. Truman, Dwight D. Eisenhower, Kim Il Sung, and Zhou Enlai. Includes bibliographical references and index.
  ISBN 1-56711-921-2 (hard : alk. paper)
  1. Korean Conflict, 1950–1953—Biography—Juvenile literature. [1. Korean Conflict, 1950–1953—Biography.] I. Title. II. Series.

CONTENTS

THE KOREAN WAR

Korea is a six-hundred-mile-long peninsula located in the eastern part of Asia, between the Sea of Japan and the Yellow Sea. It borders Russia and the People's Republic of China (Communist China) in the north and the Korean Strait in the south. Between 1950 and 1953, it was the scene of a bloody, costly war from which no country emerged victorious.

The origins of the conflict date to 1910, when Japan annexed Korea—which for centuries had been an independent country. The Japanese remained in control of Korea until the end of World War II (1939–1945). After the Japanese defeat, the country was divided at the 38th parallel (the 38th imaginary circle that spans the earth north of the equator) into two occupied zones. The Union of Soviet Socialist Republics (USSR), or Soviet Union (which then included Russia), controlled the north, while the United States had power in the south.

During World War II, the United States and the USSR had been allies. By the late 1940s, they were becoming bitter enemies. Hostilities intensified between the two

U.S. soldiers faced intense fighting from North Korean forces after entering the war.

superpowers as Harry Truman, the U.S. president, took a hard-line approach to attempts by the Soviet Union to expand its empire and spread communism across the globe. This foreign policy strategy on the part of the Communists, combined with Truman's response, ushered in the Cold War (the escalating friction between the United States and Communist bloc nations in the decades after World War II).

Korea soon became a battleground of the Cold War. In 1948, the Korean occupations ended with the establishment of separate regimes: the Communist Democratic People's Republic of Korea, or North Korea, and the Republic of Korea (ROK), or South Korea. Kim Il Sung, the North Korean president, was anxious to employ military means to unite both parts of Korea. With the support of the USSR, which provided him with armaments, he launched a surprise invasion of South Korea. At 4 A.M. on June 25, 1950, ninety thousand soldiers in the North Korean People's Army crossed the 38th parallel and advanced southward. The Korean War had begun.

The South Korean military was unprepared to defend its country, and so the United Nations (UN) Security Council quickly voted on a resolution to dispatch troops to quell the invasion. The UN forces consisted mainly of U.S. troops under the authority of U.S. commanders.

U.S. Marines make their way through destroyed buildings during the siege of the North Korean port city of Inchon.

NORTH KOREAN AGGRESSION

CHINA (Manchuria)

U.S.S.R.

Yalu River

NORTH KOREA

Pyongyang

June 25, 1950
North Korean
Communist troops
invade South Korea

June 25, 1950

38TH PARALLEL

Sea of Japan

Seoul

Inchon

Summer 1950
UN forces
occupy
Pusan
perimeter

Taejŏn

SOUTH KOREA

Mok'po

Pusan

Korea Strait

JAPAN

Capital cities
UN retreat lines
Communist drives

South Koreans welcomed U.S. troops after MacArthur's forces drove the Communists from Inchon and retook Seoul.

While the North Koreans advanced into the south and even took Seoul, the South Korean capital city, they did not win an immediate victory. The Communists suffered a major setback in September when Douglas MacArthur, supreme commander of UN forces, initiated a successful amphibious (land and sea) attack on Inchon, a North Korean port city. By the end of the month, MacArthur had reentered Seoul. UN forces then drove the Communists to the Yalu River, which bordered North Korea and Communist China.

Much to MacArthur's chagrin, the war now expanded as Communist China entered the fighting. People's Republic troops crossed into North Korea and forced MacArthur to retreat below the 38th parallel. In January 1951, they even recaptured Seoul.

In response, MacArthur wished to mount a counterattack and expand the war by invading Communist China. While the anticommunism that was at the core of Truman's foreign policy called for American involvement in Korea, the president was reluctant to authorize an offensive that would place American soldiers on Communist Chinese soil. His explanation was that he wanted to avert a major clash with the People's Republic, which possibly would lead to military confrontation with the USSR, its ally. Additionally, Truman and his top advisers believed that the Soviets were using the war as a diversionary tactic and that the greater part of America's military might should be employed to halt the spread of communism in Western Europe.

Truman's views collided with those of MacArthur. Finally, Truman elected to relieve MacArthur of his command. It was a controversial decision. MacArthur publicly chastised the president, whom he thought had forfeited all of Asia to the Communists.

Meanwhile, the Communist Chinese advance was thwarted by Matthew Ridgway, commander of the U.S. Eighth Army. Ridgway mounted a successful counterattack that pushed the Communist Chinese and North Koreans out of the south. Most significantly, he retook Seoul from the Communists. He eventually replaced MacArthur as supreme commander of UN forces.

Matthew Ridgway (front, center) eventually replaced Douglas MacArthur as the supreme commander of UN forces in the Far East.

Unlike MacArthur, Ridgway was willing to carry out Truman's policy of conducting a limited war. The fighting plodded on, and during the summer of 1951, all participants sent representatives to the Korean Armistice Conference, in which they began negotiating a cease-fire.

The peace talks lagged on through the end of 1952. By the early months of 1953, all sides recognized that the war was at a standstill and likely would end in a stalemate. Furthermore, the death of Soviet dictator Joseph Stalin in March left the USSR with an uncertain future. The Communist Chinese already had flaunted their military might in their triumph over MacArthur, while the North and South Koreans and the American public had grown weary of the war. Dwight Eisenhower, the newly elected U.S. president, also wished to end the hostilities. He achieved this by suggesting that he was considering an expansion of the war, which would include bombing

The signing of the armistice in Panmunjom initiated a cease-fire that ended the three-year conflict in Korea. A formal peace treaty was never signed.

Communist China, obstructing its ports, and even employing nuclear weapons. The fear evoked by this warning served to speed up the armistice talks.

On July 27, 1953, a cease-fire was initiated upon the signing of an armistice in the village of Panmunjom, where the negotiations had taken place. With the agreement, the North Koreans found themselves at the same spot they were in three years earlier: the 38th parallel. No formal peace treaty ever was signed. In the decades since, the North and South Koreans have viewed each other with suspicion and hostility, each hoping to one day annex the other and reunite Korea.

Reports vary on the total number of North Korean, South Korean, and Communist Chinese soldiers and civilians who were killed in the fighting. Without doubt, their numbers ran in the many hundreds of thousands, if not millions. According to the U.S. Department of Defense, 36,576 Americans died while serving in the Korean War.

STARTED WAR BY INVADING SOUTH KOREA

Kim Il Sung was born Kim Song-ju in 1912 in the northeastern Korea village of Man'gyongdae. While he was still a child, his family settled in Manchuria, located in northeastern China. He reportedly was thrown out of school and arrested at age seventeen for joining a Communist youth group. During the 1930s, Kim assisted the Chinese Communists in battling the Japanese, who had taken over Manchuria. He fled to the USSR near the beginning of World War II and spent the rest of the war in the Soviet army.

After the war, Kim returned to Korea, which by then was divided into the Soviet-occupied north and the American-occupied south. Assorted groups who had battled the Japanese were vying for control in both zones. In the north, Kim emerged as a leading contender in the power struggle. His military experience and devotion to Communist ideology had earned him respect within the USSR, and so in 1946, he was picked by the Soviet occupation commanders to head the provisional government in the north.

When North Korea became the independent Democratic People's Republic of Korea in 1948, Kim became the country's president. He quickly grew obsessed with the idea that he could unite all of Korea by using military means, and his invasion of South Korea on June 25, 1950, started the Korean War. He launched the offensive with the all-important approval of Joseph Stalin, the Soviet dictator, who provided arms for the North Korean military.

Kim felt that total victory would come within weeks. This was not to be. Stalin withdrew his backing after Douglas MacArthur, supreme commander of UN forces, landed at Inchon and drove the North Koreans to the border of the People's Republic of China (Communist China). At the signing of the Panmunjom armistice on July 27, 1953, North and South Korea again were divided at the 38th parallel. Kim's vision of a reunified Korea under his domain was shattered.

Despite this disappointment, Kim proved adept at defeating any and all political rivals in the decades after the Korean War. He remained in power until his death in 1994, reportedly from a heart attack. He was replaced as North Korean president by his son, Kim Jong Il.

Kim Il Sung, the first president of North Korea, believed that he could reunite North and South Korea through military force.

Syngman Rhee was born Yu Sung-man in 1875 in Pyongsan, a village in the Hwanghae province of Korea. After graduating from and then teaching at the Paejae Haktang, a Methodist school, he was imprisoned for opposing the Korean government. Upon his release in 1904, he went to the United States and studied at Georgetown, Harvard, and Princeton universities. In 1910, Japan took control of Korea; nine years later, Rhee, then based in Hawaii, was named first president of an independent Korean Provisional Government (or government-in-exile). Conflicts among Korean exiles in Hawaii and China resulted in his impeachment in 1925. Nevertheless, he continued to claim the title of president.

Upon Korea's liberation from Japan in 1945, Rhee returned home. However, his country was divided between the Soviet-occupied north and American-occupied south. His steadfast anti-Communist beliefs positioned him as a political force in the south. In 1948, South Korea's national assembly elected Rhee the first president of the Republic of Korea (ROK).

Rhee still was in office when South Korea was attacked by North Korea, and he led his country throughout the war. After the invasion, his army was ill equipped to retaliate—or even defend itself—and UN forces had to

Syngman Rhee (left) served as the president of South Korea throughout the war, receiving vital help from UN forces (above) in defending his country against the Communist invasion.

be dispatched to secure South Korea. Rhee nonetheless hoped that the fighting would end with a reunified Korea, under his leadership. He became increasingly tyrannical. He clashed with the UN over who should control liberated North Korean territory and placed Pusan, the wartime South Korean capital, under martial law (replacing civil authority with military force). While he did not come to rule all of Korea at war's end, his power in South Korea was absolute.

Rhee remained in office throughout the 1950s, then resigned the presidency after a massive student protest of his attempt to fix the 1960 presidential election. He went into exile in Hawaii, where he died in 1965 after suffering a stroke.

HARRY S. TRUMAN

Harry S. Truman was born in Lamar, Missouri, in 1884. He served with the Missouri Field Artillery in World War I (1914–1918), won a judgeship in Jackson County, Missouri, in 1922, and became a U.S. senator in 1934. In 1944, he was the Democratic Party vice presidential running mate of President Franklin Roosevelt in his successful reelection bid. Upon Roosevelt's sudden death in 1945, Truman became the thirty-third U.S. president. He narrowly won the 1948 election and began a second term that was dominated by the Korean War.

Truman's tough-on-communism approach to foreign affairs was articulated in his Truman Doctrine, a 1947 policy statement in which he pledged to assist countries endangered by Communist expansion. This course of action gave Truman justification for agreeing to send U.S. troops to fight in Korea.

Conversely, Truman remained unwilling to sanction a military offensive that would place American forces on Communist Chinese soil. His rationale was that he wished to avoid a showdown with the People's Republic—and, conceivably, the Soviet Union. This strategy clashed with the view of Douglas MacArthur, supreme commander of UN forces, who wanted to lead his armies into China. Truman's decision to relieve MacArthur of his command was one of his most controversial war-related actions. It placed the president directly at odds with his political enemies and staunch anti-Communists, who believed that by ousting MacArthur the president was conceding defeat to the Communists not only in Korea but throughout Asia.

The American public's increasing apprehension over the pace and course of the war, as well as inflation, incidences of government corruption, and increasing fears about the threat of communism on the home front, resulted in a steep decline in Truman's popularity. His Republican political enemies exploited all these issues, and also insisted on an absolute defeat of the Communists in Korea. In 1952, with his approval rating at an all-time low of 23 percent, Truman declared that he would not run for reelection.

Truman retired to Independence, Missouri, where he wrote his memoirs and helped develop the Truman Presidential Museum and Library. He died of heart failure and complications from old age in 1972.

President Harry Truman pledged to assist countries threatened by communism. His 1947 Truman Doctrine justified his sending U.S. troops to South Korea.

ZHOU ENLAI

Zhou Enlai was born in 1898 in Huai'an, in the Chinese province of Jiangsu. He studied in Paris, Japan, and his homeland, and during the late 1910s and early 1920s became a Marxist (a devotee of the philosophy of communism developed during the mid-nineteenth century by Karl Marx and Friedrich Engels). From the late 1920s on, he was a central figure in Chinese Communist Party politics. In 1949, he became prime minister of the newly established Communist People's Republic of China after Mao Zedong and his Red Army drove the non-Communist Chinese off the mainland to the island of Formosa.

In his capacity as prime minister, Zhou was a major force in establishing and implementing People's Republic foreign policy before and during the Korean War. In 1950, he negotiated and signed a treaty with the USSR, which allied these two Communist powers. Upon North Korea's invasion of the south, he initially was against Communist Chinese involvement in the conflict. Primarily, he wished to avoid battling a superior American military and instead focus on building his country's economy. His strategy changed when, reportedly at the request of the Soviets, he warned that he would send troops to Korea if the American military crossed the 38th parallel.

The United States and UN ignored Zhou's threat and mounted a counterattack that drove the North Koreans to the border between North Korea and Communist

UN soldiers stand guard over Chinese prisoners of war (above). Chinese prime minister Zhou Enlai (left) sent troops to help the North Koreans.

China. At that point, the People's Republic entered the war, resulting in confrontation and combat between American and Chinese troops.

Throughout the fighting, Zhou delivered countless denouncements of the presence of the United States and UN in the region. The People's Republic was not a member of the UN, which Zhou claimed was little more than a political arm of the United States.

After the war, Zhou remained prime minister of the People's Republic until his death from cancer in 1976.

Joseph Stalin was born Iosif Vissarionovich Dzhugashvili in 1879 in the town of Gori, in what then was the Russian colony of Georgia. As a young man, he embraced Marxism and became a high-profile pro-Communist activist and organizer. After the 1917–1920 Russian Revolution and civil war, from which the Communists emerged victorious, he consolidated his power base within the Russian Communist Party. In 1929, he became dictator of the Soviet Union.

Stalin ruled the USSR at the end of World War II, when Korea was divided at the 38th parallel and occupied by the Soviets in the north and the Americans in the south. While he was eager to see Communist expansion across the globe, he also wanted to avoid direct confrontation with the United States and heartily supported North Korea's plan to attack the south.

The Soviet dictator assumed that Americans would be weary of fighting so soon after World War II and would shun involvement in the conflict. He also believed that all of Korea would rapidly merge as a united Communist state.

Stalin severely miscalculated on both counts. The American people were prepared to support a war against communism and backed Harry Truman's decision to send troops into battle. Then the Soviets made an even bigger blunder. At the time, the Communist People's Republic of China was not a part of the UN. The Soviets had been unsuccessfully endorsing the People's Republic—its political ally—for UN membership. As the UN Security Council was set to vote on a resolution to dispatch troops to Korea, the Soviet representative was instructed to boycott Security Council meetings because the council had declined to seat the Communist Chinese delegates. For this reason, the Soviets were unable to employ their veto power and prevent the UN from authorizing the military defense of South Korea. Furthermore, the North Koreans enjoyed no quick victory in the south.

Stalin eventually withdrew his backing of the war after Douglas MacArthur, supreme commander of UN forces, landed at Inchon and drove the North Koreans to the Chinese border. He remained a behind-the-scenes force, though, as he reportedly encouraged Communist China's entry into the conflict.

Stalin still was dictator of the USSR when he died of a cerebral hemorrhage in March 1953, almost five months before the cease-fire that ended the Korean War.

Joseph Stalin encouraged North Korea to invade the south because he supported Communist expansion across the globe.

DEAN ACHESON

U.S. SECRETARY OF STATE

Dean Gooderham Acheson was born in Middletown, Connecticut, in 1893. He attended Yale University, served in the U.S. Navy, and graduated from Harvard University Law School. He then worked as a law clerk for U.S. Supreme Court justice Louis Brandeis and eventually became a partner in Covington & Burling, a Washington, D.C., law firm. He was assistant secretary of state during World War II and advanced to undersecretary of state upon Harry Truman's assumption of the U.S. presidency. Truman named Acheson secretary of state in 1949.

Acheson was one of the president's most trusted advisers and a major architect of American foreign policy. The cornerstone of his stance was that the USSR had to be thwarted in its attempt to spread its Communist ideology to other nations. This philosophy and Acheson's belief that the Soviets had initiated the attack on South Korea played a major role in Truman's decision to become directly involved in the conflict in Korea.

Acheson staunchly urged the UN Security Council to condemn the North Korean attack on the South and intervene militarily in the crisis. He reassured America's European allies, who were concerned that the escalating conflict would lead to nuclear war, and eventually backed Truman's decision to remove Douglas MacArthur as the supreme commander of UN forces after the general publicly stated his desire to lead his troops into Communist China.

While he advocated U.S. involvement in Korea, Acheson accepted the notion that the conflict might end in a stalemate. Furthermore, he believed that the greater part of America's military resources would be better utilized to combat the threat of communism in Western Europe. His rationale was that U.S. security and prosperity were most directly connected to the preservation of freedom in the Western European nations. This view made him a controversial figure, as his political opponents felt he was far too indulgent in his policies against Chinese Communist aggression.

After Truman left office in 1953, Acheson returned to private law practice but also remained a high-profile political adviser who supported a tough, military-oriented anti-Soviet foreign policy. He died of a stroke in 1971.

Secretary of State Dean Acheson believed the U.S. military should concentrate on fighting communism in Western Europe instead of in Korea.

Joseph Raymond McCarthy was born in Appleton, Wisconsin, in 1908. He graduated from Marquette University in Milwaukee, began a modest career as a lawyer, joined the Republican Party and won a Circuit Court judgeship, and served in the U.S. Marines during World War II. He was elected to the U.S. Senate in 1946.

McCarthy, an archconservative, was at the forefront of the anti-Communist hysteria that gripped the United States during the post–World War II era and only increased as the Korean War lumbered on. He alleged that the war effort was being undermined by traitorous Democratic Party policy makers who were "soft on communism."

One such policy maker was Dean Acheson, Harry Truman's secretary of state. Acheson felt that Russia and China were natural adversaries despite their shared political ideologies, and he believed that discord inevitably would develop between the two Communist superpowers. Because of these beliefs, Acheson felt that the United States should focus on containing communism in Western Europe while remaining on the sidelines with regard to China. In response, McCarthy alleged that Acheson was far too lenient in his policies against non-Soviet Communist movements and that he did not act to prevent the Communists from taking over mainland China and safeguard American interests in Asia. McCarthy claimed that Acheson's highly publicized views only encouraged Kim Il Sung to invade South Korea. Another McCarthy target was George Marshall, Truman's former secretary of state, who became secretary of defense in 1950. Marshall was a respected statesman and soldier who had been the U.S. Army chief of staff during World War II. As defense secretary, he was entrusted with increasing military manpower and firepower in Europe, as well as Korea, and ensuring that the State and Defense Departments worked in tandem. McCarthy alleged that Marshall's decisions supported the Communists. He also insinuated that Marshall was a traitor—a charge that was preposterous, given Marshall's long history of distinguished service to his country.

After the Korean War ended in a stalemate, McCarthy continued his anti-Communist offensive. In 1953, he began an investigation of supposed Communist

Senator Joseph McCarthy believed Democratic Party policy makers undermined the war effort with their soft stance on communism.

REPUBLICAN
JOSEPH R.
McCARTHY
FOR
U. S.
SENATOR

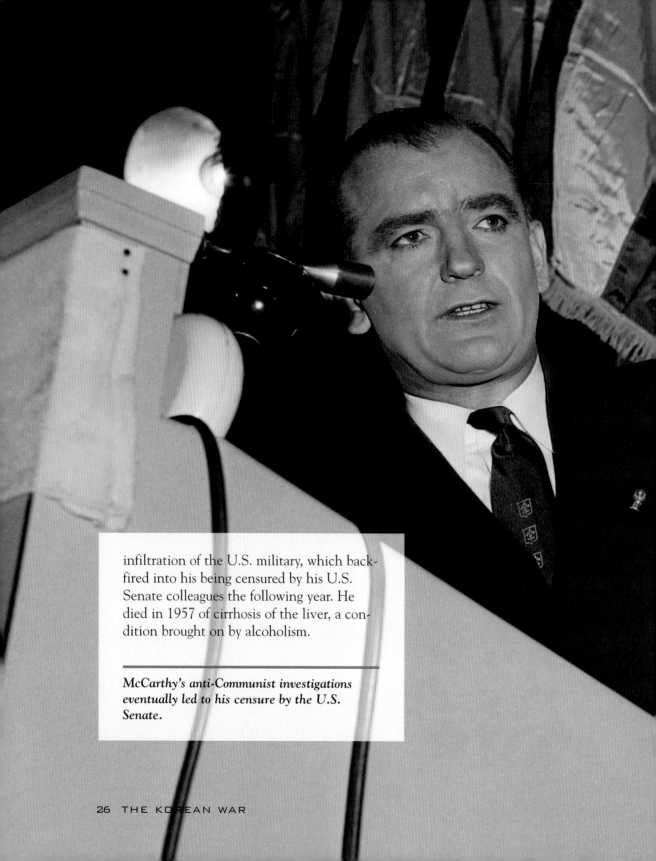

infiltration of the U.S. military, which back-
fired into his being censured by his U.S.
Senate colleagues the following year. He
died in 1957 of cirrhosis of the liver, a con-
dition brought on by alcoholism.

McCarthy's anti-Communist investigations
eventually led to his censure by the U.S.
Senate.

Omar Nelson Bradley was born in Clark, Missouri, in 1893. He graduated from the U.S. Military Academy at West Point and served in various posts in the U.S. Army from the mid-1910s to the beginning of World War II. During the war, he was most prominent as commander of the U.S. First Army and Twelfth Army groups in European operations. Afterward, he headed the Veterans Administration and was the U.S. Army chief of staff.

In 1949, Bradley became the first chairman of the joint chiefs of staff, a position he held throughout the Korean War. In this capacity, he was the top-ranked American military officer. Before the war began, Bradley paid little attention to Korea. However, he viewed North Korea's invasion as a chance for the United States to aggressively take action against the Communists. With UN approval, he and the joint chiefs dispatched American troops to assist the South Koreans.

Chairman of the Joint Chiefs of Staff Omar Bradley (left) sent U.S. troops to South Korea (above). He advised President Truman to fight only on the Korean peninsula.

Throughout the war, Bradley continuously counseled Harry Truman. He was the president's most valued military consultant and played a major role in devising military strategy as the war developed. While supporting U.S. participation in the war, Bradley also advised Truman to restrict the fighting to the Korean peninsula and not approve an advance into Communist Chinese territory. He believed that the Soviets were using the war as a diversionary tactic and were hoping that U.S. involvement in Korea would obscure their primary aim: to spread communism throughout Western Europe. He even went before the U.S. Congress to endorse Truman's policy of limiting the war.

Bradley left the joint chiefs in August 1953, less than a month after the signing of the armistice that ended the Korean War. He became chairman of the board of the Bulova Watch Company and remained an adviser to American presidents until his death from a blood clot on the brain in 1981.

Douglas MacArthur was born in Little Rock, Arkansas, in 1880. He graduated first in his class from the U.S. Military Academy at West Point, commanded the Forty-second Rainbow Division during World War I, and afterward served as superintendent of West Point and U.S. Army chief of staff. He retired in 1937 but was recalled to active duty in 1941 to command U.S. military forces in the Far East. During World War II, he was Allied supreme commander of the southwest Pacific arena. At war's end, he supervised the reconstruction of U.S.-occupied Japan.

MacArthur's actions as a military leader in Korea greatly impacted the direction of the war. At its outset, he was named supreme commander of UN forces. After containing the Communist offensive, he instigated a successful counterattack that culminated in his trouncing the North Koreans behind enemy lines at Inchon. He then pressed forward against the Communists, driving them to the border between North Korea and Communist China.

The war seemed nearly over to MacArthur, but he overlooked the prospect that the Chinese might respond to his actions. They in fact dispatched substantial numbers of troops into battle against his armies, which were compelled to retreat.

An irritated and embarrassed MacArthur publicly proclaimed his determination to lead his forces into Communist China. This strategy put him at odds with Harry Truman, who wished to limit American participation in the war to the Korean peninsula. The president ordered MacArthur to discontinue releasing public declarations that conflicted with presidential policy. Eventually, he relieved MacArthur of his command.

MacArthur was convinced that Truman had conceded all of Asia to the Communists. Upon his return home, he criticized the president while speaking before a joint session of the U.S. Congress and continued his condemnation in public appearances across the country.

MacArthur's battlefield triumphs, combined with his open defiance of Truman, made him one of the most celebrated and controversial of all twentieth-century American military leaders. He eventually became chairman of the board of the Remington Rand Corporation and died in 1964 after suffering liver and kidney malfunctions.

UN supreme commander Douglas MacArthur's intention to lead his forces into Communist China conflicted with President Truman's foreign policy.

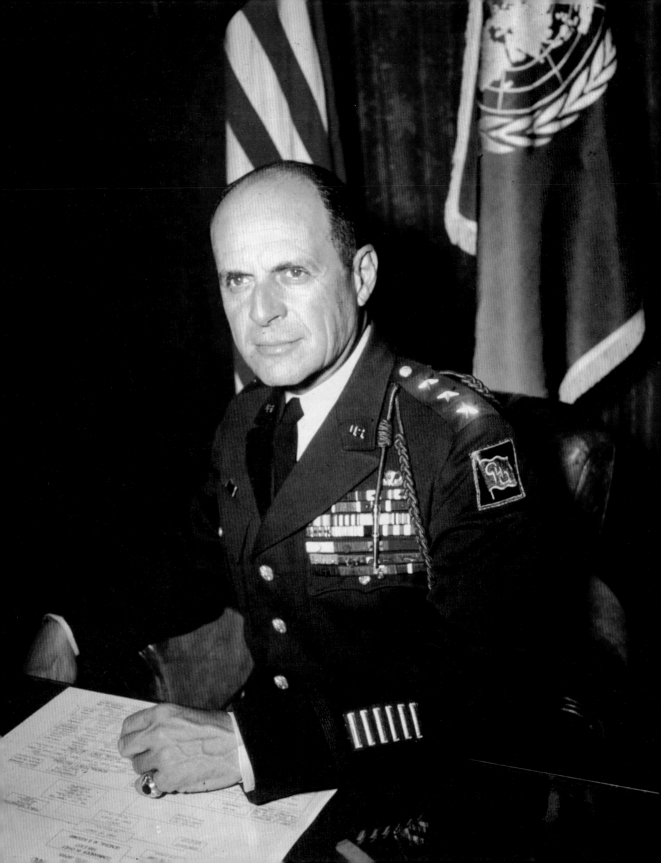

MATTHEW RIDGWAY

Matthew Bunker Ridgway was born in 1895 in Fort Monroe, Virginia. He graduated from the U.S. Military Academy at West Point, served in various capacities in the U.S. Army between the late 1910s and 1930s, and during World War II led the Eighty-second Airborne Division in combat across Europe. During the immediate postwar years, he served in the Mediterranean and Caribbean and was named U.S. Army deputy chief of staff.

Ridgway's brilliance as a motivator and strategist was the key component to his rallying UN and South Korean forces in Korea. He took command of the U.S. Eighth Army in late 1950, replacing General Walton Walker, who had been killed in a Jeep mishap. At the time, the Communist Chinese were advancing against Douglas MacArthur's forces, which had retreated back into South Korea. The Chinese had devastated the U.S. First Cavalry and Second Infantry divisions, not to mention the South Korean military—which reportedly was contemplating laying down its arms. Ridgway revitalized his troops by reminding them of their all-important mission: to halt the spread of communism in South Korea.

Ridgway initiated "Operation Killer," a cleverly devised counterattack. The Communists were assaulted by a massive force consisting of over one hundred thousand troops in eight infantry divisions, supported by five tank and twenty-two artillery battalions and the full power of the U.S. Air Force. The counterattack succeeded in pushing the North Koreans and Chinese out of South Korea, thus subverting what then seemed to be a surefire Communist victory. The following year, Ridgway replaced Douglas MacArthur as the supreme commander of UN forces. In this capacity, he commanded all U.S. and UN fighting units in Korea. Unlike MacArthur, who advocated an all-out offensive into Communist China, Ridgway was content to carry out Harry Truman's policy and conduct a limited war. Eventually, the president reassigned him to Europe, where he also served as supreme allied commander.

After the war, Ridgway was named U.S. Army chief of staff. He served in this post until his retirement in 1955. He then worked in the private business community and died of cardiac arrest in 1993.

Matthew Ridgway's counterattack pushed the Communist Chinese and North Koreans out of South Korea.

James Alward Van Fleet was born in 1892 in Coytesville, New Jersey. He graduated from the U.S. Military Academy at West Point, directed a machine-gun battalion in France during World War I, and commanded several U.S. fighting divisions throughout Europe during World War II. Then he helped organize and train the Greek military, which successfully resisted Communist guerrillas.

Van Fleet conducted major military offensives for the United States during the Korean War. In April 1951, he replaced Matthew Ridgway as commander of the U.S. Eighth Army. At that juncture, the Communist Chinese and North Koreans were about to begin their most ambitious military offensive. The Eighth Army was entrenched at the 38th parallel when the Communists attacked. Van Fleet's skillful maneuvering of his troops resulted in seventy thousand enemy casualties—and a successful defense of the front line.

After a second, lesser Communist offensive in May, Van Fleet launched his own offensive, leading his forces to the Iron Triangle region north of the 38th parallel and inflicting two hundred thousand casualties on the Communists. At that point, Ridgway—who had replaced Douglas MacArthur as the supreme commander of UN forces—ordered Van Fleet to halt the advance. Ridgway felt the Eighth Army lacked sufficient manpower to prolong the attack. Van Fleet agreed, but eventually asserted that continuing the offensive might have resulted in total victory against the Communists. He subsequently led other smaller offensives but was ordered to halt them amid the increasing likelihood that the war would end in a truce.

Van Fleet's participation in the war was not confined to the battlefield. He established innovative training programs for the South Korean military, which was transformed into an impressive fighting force. He even came to be known as "The Father of the Korean Army."

His growing frustration over the manner in which his superiors were handling the war caused Van Fleet to relinquish his command in February 1953. He left the military in April. After the war, Van Fleet worked in real estate and served several presidential administrations as an adviser and special ambassador. He died in his sleep in 1992, five months after his one hundredth birthday.

After taking command of the Eighth Army, General James Van Fleet launched an offensive north of the 38th parallel that resulted in heavy Communist casualties.

Paik Sun Yup was born in 1920 in Kangseo, a small town in northern Korea. He attended the Mukden Military Academy in Manchuria and served in the Manchurian army during World War II. An anti-Communist, he settled in South Korea at war's end and joined the South Korean Constabulary, which was converted into the Republic of Korea (ROK) Army in 1948.

During the Korean War, Paik earned respect as a knowledgeable and daring military leader. At the war's outset, he was commander of the ROK's First Infantry Division. In August 1950, he and his soldiers were charged with protecting a roadway that led into Tabudong, a South Korean village. Meanwhile, the Twenty-seventh Infantry Regiment was positioned as support troops. During a battle against the North Koreans, the Twenty-seventh was surrounded by the enemy and about to retreat. Paik personally intervened by coming to the front line and leading the Twenty-seventh in a successful counterattack.

The following year, Paik was put in command of the ROK I Corps. The corps was sorely in need of artillery, and he employed his organizational skills to best utilize all available weaponry. That November, he led the corps in a campaign to halt North Korean guerilla activity in the Chiri Mountains, in the southwestern portion of South Korea. Four months later, at the operation's conclusion, the corps had killed or captured twenty-five thousand

South Korean commander Paik Sun Yup (left, center) led his forces in several successful campaigns. Paik (above, second from right) became South Korea's first four-star military leader.

guerrillas. The I Corps eventually was renamed Task Force Paik.

In 1952, Paik became commander of the newly created ROK II Corps. That July, he was named the ROK Army chief of staff and represented South Korea at the cease-fire negotiations. Upon his promotion to general in 1953, he became the first four-star South Korean military officer.

After the war, Paik continued his military career, which culminated in his becoming chairman of the ROK joint chiefs of staff. He left the armed forces in 1960 and entered the South Korean diplomatic service before retiring to Seoul, the South Korean capital city.

LED COMMUNIST CHINESE MILITARY OPERATIONS

Peng Dehuai was born in 1898 in Shixiang, a village in the Hunan Province of China. After serving in a regional warlord's army, he graduated from the Hunan Military Academy and in 1928 joined the Communist Party. During World War II, he led both Communist and non-Communist Chinese into battle against the Japanese. Afterward, he emerged a military commander in the Chinese Civil War that concluded with the Communists taking over the Chinese mainland in 1949.

Upon Communist China's entry into the Korean War, Peng became supreme commander of the Chinese People's Volunteers, his country's military force. His aim was to take all of South Korea; his immediate mission was to rescue North Korea in the wake of Douglas MacArthur's victory at Inchon and the successful drive of the North Koreans to the Yalu River at the North Korean–Chinese border.

Peng Dehuai (right) used the overwhelming manpower of the Chinese army to push UN forces (above) to Seoul.

Peng compensated for his lack of military hardware by skillfully employing his one asset: an endless supply of manpower. His 380,000-man army forded the Yalu and began an offensive against MacArthur's troops. Between October 1950 and January 1951, the Volunteers on three occasions struck the UN forces, eventually pushing them back below the 38th parallel. During this offensive, in what would be his greatest battlefield triumph, Peng captured Seoul, the South Korean capital city. The Volunteers later relinquished Seoul to Matthew Ridgway, who had replaced MacArthur as the supreme commander of UN forces.

In addition to leading all of Communist China's military operations, Peng was charged with communicating with the leaders of North Korea and the Soviet Union. He was the People's Republic representative who signed the armistice that ended the war.

From 1954 to 1959, Peng served as Communist China's minister of defense. He was forced to relinquish this post after unsuccessfully opposing the economic and military policies of the country's top leadership. He was placed under house arrest and eventually was reportedly sent to prison, where he died of a liver disorder in 1974.

DWIGHT D. EISENHOWER

Dwight David Eisenhower was born in Denison, Texas, in 1890. He graduated from the U.S. Military Academy at West Point and, across the decades, rose within the ranks of the U.S. Army. He was supreme commander of Allied troops in Europe during World War II and led the military campaigns that resulted in the German surrender. After the war, he commanded the American occupation force in Germany and later served as president of Columbia University.

At the outset of the Korean War, Harry Truman named Eisenhower supreme commander of the armed forces of the North Atlantic Treaty Organization (NATO), which united non-Communist nations in North America and Western Europe in the event of an armed Communist attack. However, as the 1952 Republican Party presidential nominee, Eisenhower criticized the overall manner in which Truman, a Democrat, had managed the war. He promised that, if elected, he would visit Korea and personally scrutinize the situation. This tactic appealed to U.S. voters, who by then had become weary of the stalemated war. On election day, Eisenhower trounced Adlai Stevenson, the Democratic candidate, and became the thirty-fourth U.S. president.

Eisenhower's decisions directly led to the end of the war. First, the president-elect flew to Korea and conferred with Mark Clark, who had succeeded Matthew Ridgway as supreme commander of UN forces, and Syngman Rhee, the South Korean president. Both urged him to expand the fighting. However, Eisenhower also extensively interviewed American troops and came away with an awareness of their low morale and their increased questioning of the war's purpose.

Eisenhower returned home determined to end the war, but not by sanctioning an offensive or withdrawing U.S. troops. He accomplished this by hinting that he was pondering an expansion of the war, which included bombing Communist China, blockading its ports, and even using nuclear weapons. Such threats hastened the ongoing armistice talks, which involved all the war's participants. Six months after Eisenhower entered office, on July 27, 1953, the Panmunjom armistice was signed. Eisenhower was reelected in 1956 and served out his second term as president. He retired in 1961 and died of heart failure in 1969.

Presidential candidate Dwight Eisenhower's criticism of President Harry Truman's handling of the war resulted in Eisenhower's election to the presidency in 1952.

C. TURNER JOY

COMMANDER OF AMERICAN NAVAL FORCES

Charles Turner Joy was born in St. Louis, Missouri, in 1895. He graduated from the U.S. Naval Academy at Annapolis and was commissioned an ensign in the U.S. Navy. He later attended the University of Michigan, commanded his first navy battleship in 1933, and returned to the Naval Academy as an administrator. During World War II, he most notably saw combat as a ship commander in the Pacific.

At the outset of the Korean War, Joy was commander of American naval forces in the Far East. Despite his conviction that his forces would be unable to halt the North Korean attack, Joy was able to utilize his resources and support his personnel in combat during the war's early months. Initially, he did not favor a plan by Douglas MacArthur, supreme commander of UN forces, to attack the North Koreans behind enemy lines at Inchon. Once it became clear that the offensive was essential to the containment of the enemy, Joy wholeheartedly offered his support.

C. Turner Joy (second from left) served as the chief UN representative at peace talks with the Communists in the summer of 1951.

Most significantly, Joy participated in the armistice conference that led to the end of the war. In July 1951, when the fighting was at a standstill, he was named chief and senior representative of the UN command delegation. In this capacity, he represented the UN in peace talks with the Communists.

Joy believed that only the threat of absolute military force would induce the Communists to earnestly negotiate. It was a strategy that the United States and UN were unwilling to employ. Joy felt that the lack of such a threat convinced the Communists that they could stretch out the discussions and win additional concessions. His dissatisfaction over the direction of the negotiations caused him to resign from the delegation in May 1952, fourteen months before the signing of the armistice. Ironically, after becoming U.S. president, Dwight D. Eisenhower accelerated the armistice talks by suggesting that he might expand the war—the same tactic that Joy had unsuccessfully advocated.

After the war, Joy became superintendent of the U.S. Naval Academy. He died of leukemia in 1956.

Admiral C. Turner Joy believed that only the threat of military force would make the Communists willing to negotiate in peace talks.

1945, August 15	U.S. president Harry Truman and USSR dictator Joseph Stalin agree that upon the end of World War II, Korea will be temporarily divided at the 38th parallel. The Soviets will occupy the north, while the U.S. will occupy the south.
September 9	The Japanese surrender in Korea.
1948	Syngman Rhee becomes president of the Republic of Korea (ROK), or South Korea. The North Korean Supreme People's Assembly names Kim Il Sung the country's president.
1950, May	Kim Il Sung meets with Stalin and leaders of the People's Republic of China (Communist China) seeking their support for an invasion of South Korea.
June 25	North Korea invades South Korea. The Korean War begins.
June 27	Seoul, the South Korean capital city, falls to the North Koreans. The UN Security Council meets in an emergency session, votes to condemn the North Korean invasion, and sanctions sending troops to South Korea to quell the attack.
June 30	President Harry S. Truman commits U.S. troops to the war.
July 7	Douglas MacArthur is named supreme commander of UN forces in Korea.
August 7	MacArthur begins his counterattack against the North Koreans.
September 15	Under MacArthur's command, 25,000 U.S. Marines land at Inchon, located 200 miles behind North Korean lines.
September 19–29	Seoul is recaptured; MacArthur and Rhee enter the city.
September 30	Zhou Enlai, prime minister of the People's Republic of China, advises UN forces to steer clear of the Yalu River, which borders North Korea and Communist China.

October 5	Peng Dehuai is named supreme commander of the Chinese People's Volunteers, Communist China's military force.
October 8	MacArthur's forces cross the 38th parallel and begin making their way to the Yalu River.
October 14–18	Peng's forces cross the Yalu River into North Korea and begin their campaign against UN forces.
November 25	UN and South Korean forces begin their retreat from the north to below the 38th parallel.
1951, January 3	The Chinese People's Volunteers recapture Seoul.
February 18–March 17	Matthew Ridgway, commander of the U.S. Eighth Army, launches "Operation Killer," a successful counterattack against the North Koreans and Communist Chinese.
March 18	UN forces retake Seoul.
April 11	Truman dismisses Douglas MacArthur as supreme commander of UN forces. MacArthur is replaced by Ridgway.
April 15	James Van Fleet takes command of the U.S. Eighth Army.
April 19	MacArthur appears before the U.S. Congress and criticizes Truman's handling of the war.
April 22–29	The U.S. Eighth Army repels the Communists at the 38th parallel and begins advancing into the north.
June–July	Van Fleet is ordered to halt his attack in the wake of the beginning of truce negotiations.
July 10	The Korean Armistice Conference begins. Peace talks will continue for the next two years.
1953, January 20	Dwight Eisenhower replaces Harry Truman as U.S. president.
March 5	Joseph Stalin, the Soviet dictator, dies.
July 27	The UN command, the North Korean Army, and the Chinese People's Volunteers sign a military armistice agreement that ends the hostilities in Korea.

FOR FURTHER INFORMATION

BOOKS

Sonia G. Benson, *Korean War*. Detroit: U*X*L, 2001.

Linda Granfield, *I Remember Korea: Veterans Tell Their Stories of the Korean War 1950–53*. New York: Clarion, 2003.

Maurice Isserman and John Bowman, *Korean War*. New York: Facts On File, 2003.

Michael Uschan, *The Korean War*. San Diego: Lucent, 2001.

Diane Yancey, *Life of an American Soldier*. San Diego: Lucent, 2003.

Jeff C. Young, *The Korean War*. Berkeley Heights, NJ: MyReportLinks.com, 2003.

WEB SITES

Examining the Korean War
http://mcel.pacificu.edu/as/students/stanley/home.html
Web site "designed to educate readers about the Korean War and to offer resources for learning and research."

Korean War
www.kimsoft.com/kr-war.htm
All-purpose Web site offering information on the war and links to scores of Korean War–related Web resources.

Korean War Veterans Memorial
www.nps.gov/kowa
Web page sponsored by the National Park Service, U.S. Department of the Interior, spotlighting the Korean War Veterans Memorial in Washington, D.C.

About the Author

Rob Edelman is a writer who lives with his wife, Audrey Kupferberg, in Amsterdam, New York. He has authored several books on baseball and movie and television personalities, and teaches film history at the University of Albany. He enjoys watching old movies and attending baseball games.